Little Iguana

By Carmie Ruiz   **Illustrated by Sheila Bailey**

Target Skill Short *Ii*/i/

PEARSON

Scott
Foresman

iguana

We have a little iguana.

3

igloo

We have a little igloo.

It is for the little iguana.

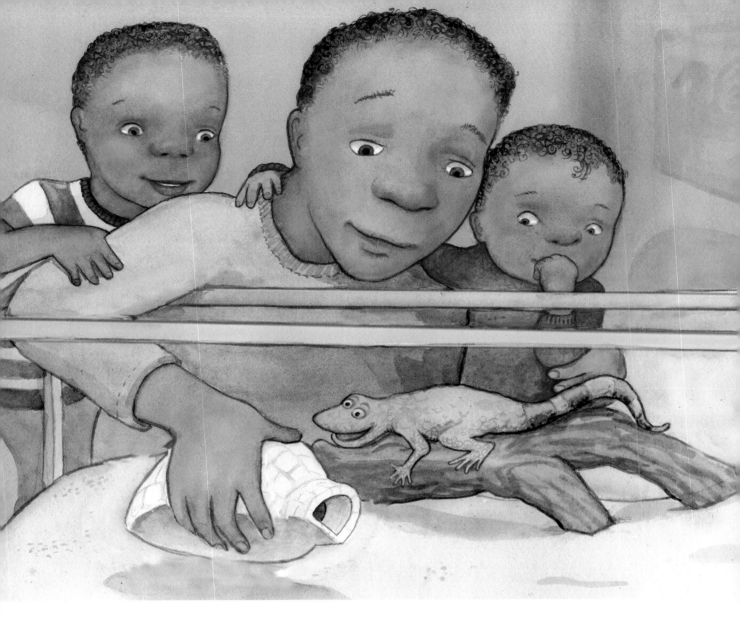

He likes the little igloo.

We like the little iguana.